POEMS THAT SPARK DISCUSSION

PTSD

One Veterans quest to find his voice and
manage Post Traumatic Stress Disorder (PTSD)

WAYNE D FEDERATION

Be Wayfedration

 Friesenpress

Suite 300 - 990 Fort St
Victoria, BC, V8V 3K2
Canada

www.friesenpress.com

Author: Ed Brown

Introduction by Chris Linford LCol (retired) COPE Director
Major Jack Thurgar SC MBE OAM RFD (Ret'd)
and Dr. Sana-Ara Ahmed, MD FRCPC Anesthesiologist &
Cannabinoid Medicine Specialist

ISBN
978-1-5255-0860-8 (Hardcover)
978-1-5255-0861-5 (Paperback)
978-1-5255-0862-2 (eBook)

1. SELF-HELP, POST-TRAUMATIC STRESS DISORDER (PTSD)

Distributed to the trade by The Ingram Book Company

DEDICATION

This book is dedicated to all survivors of PTSD, their significant others, support staff and friends. PTSD is a battle that cannot be fought alone. I thank you.

I also dedicate this book to those who did not make it.

FOREWORD I

Wayne Federation is a man who seeks peace. He has lived a full life and served his country well.

Sadly, when we choose to take on such missions, we can often find ourselves in nasty places and witness to some nasty things. Wayne takes us on a journey with him as he delicately arranges the words in a way that most would not. This short, concise prose allowed me to digest the content in a way that gave me permission to ponder and truly take in what Wayne was expressing.

No subject is off the record for Wayne and that's why I enjoyed this collection so much. I have never been a huge fan of poetry, but I found myself travelling from one to another, wondering what the next would be like. I found myself identifying with the premise several times, which made me sad, happy, full of sorrow and again back to happy. It was a bit of a roller coaster for me, but I enjoyed it very much.

This collection of poetry by Wayne Federation is a gift; please read it once, and then again, as one misses things the first time through.

Thank you very much, Wayne, for your honesty and willingness to publicly embrace your vulnerability. This has made you stronger and will allow you to stay the course along with Dianne, for life!

Chris Linford, Lieutenant-Colonel (Retired)
COPE Director

FOREWORD II

The title of this book of poems, *Poems That Spark Discussion*, by Wayne Federation CD, BSc, not only defines the concept and experiences of a soldier who suffers from Post-Traumatic Stress Disorder (PTSD), but also it allows his partner to verbalize how her husband's condition has affected her and their relationship.

The writing of a poem is very difficult as it is exposes one's innermost thoughts and feelings, laying one's soul bare, so to speak. It is unlocking and opening up a door which houses 'secrets' one has guarded and is afraid to expose to the light of day – lest they be discovered, talked about and ridiculed by non-understanding others. These poems cut to the very core of who the author is and what he has endured and suffered and its effect upon those close to him who love him and still need him, even though he sometimes thinks he is 'worthless' and not worthy of being loved for what he has or has not done in his military career.

Governments have known, yet denied the medical condition now referred to as PTSD since WWI. Captain JC Dunn, DCM MC, a Medical Officer serving with the 2nd Battalion the Royal Welch Fusiliers, wrote of life in the trenches in his book: *The War the Infantry Knew*. Two literary giants of the last century served in that unit and wrote of their experiences on the Western Front within that book. Captain Siegfried Sassoon MC and Captain Robert Graves. They, in their own way, spoke from the heart – just as Wayne does here.

For me, Wayne has verbalized many of the interfering and dark thoughts that steal their way into one's consciousness daily. He writes of self-doubt, despair, suicide, depression, anger, self-medication on drugs, violent outbursts, and the ever-pervading feeling of 'hopelessness' accompanied by unexplainable lethargy – all of which is the burden of the sufferer of PTSD.

Yet among all the garbage on the scrapheap of life, Wayne finds goodness, hope and the desire to live. This desire is promoted within Wayne by education about his condition, the love, understanding, and fortitude of his partner Dianne; a belief in God; and the desire to inspire and help fellow sufferers of PTSD through his writings.

Having experienced PTSD on a personal level after active service in Vietnam as a Special Forces soldier (Australian SASR) and later in Cyprus as an Australian Police Officer attached to various Canadian Contingents, (including Lord Strathcona's Horse (Royal Canadians)), where I worked closely with Wayne, I can say that this book of poems is 'right on the money'.

I commend this excellent book – *Poems That Spark Discussion* especially to: those who suffer from PTSD; their partners (or ex-partners); their parents, children; and to those health-care professionals working in this field, and to the general public who wish to learn and understand 'the price paid' by many modern-day Canadian Warriors.

Major Jack Thurgar
SC MBE OAM RFD (Retired)

WAYNE D FEDERATION

FOREWORD III

Wayne is a success story from my practice. Our first meeting in Spring 2016 started an educational and mutually beneficial journey exploring the benefits of medical cannabis as a sole option for therapeutic management of pain and anxiety. The practice of pain management is at a cross roads given the epidemic of addiction and overdose deaths from prescription opioid medications in Canada. There truly is a need for an alternative option. Despite being slowed by legal restrictions and stigma; medical cannabis is relatively non-addicting and has the best safety record of any pain medication known and is an excellent alternative. Wayne's determination to solely use medical cannabis as his therapeutic solution, has pushed me as a doctor in my knowledge about treating pain with cannabis. My understanding about cannabinoid deficiencies in pain states and post-traumatic stress states has grown and I have developed therapeutic regimens using delta-tetrahydrocannabinol (THC) and cannabidiol (CBD) to treat the constellation of symptoms of depression, anxiety, insomnia, and pain together.

It is with great pleasure and honor that I write an introduction for Wayne and his collection of poetry that depicts the human suffering, which occurs in war and conflict. As one reads these poems, one embarks on a journey of longing, confusion, suffering and ultimately redemption and freedom. Wayne gut-wrenchingly shares his depth and honour as a soldier and the long-lasting impact it has had on himself and his family. I encourage you as a reader, to follow along and discover the turning point Wayne goes through in his understanding and treatment of post-traumatic stress disorder (PTSD) and his victory as he achieves peace once more.

Post-Traumatic Stress Disorder (PTSD) is a psychiatric disorder of significant prevalence in war veterans and war survivors. The pathogenesis of PTSD is understood to be a paradoxical change in emotional memory processing. Cannabinoid research suggests a link between endocannabinoid deficiencies and maladaptive brain changes after trauma exposures.[1] The role of the endocannabinoid system is to regulate mood states and participate in memory consolidation, retrieval, and extinction. Clinical findings show a positive relationship between THC use and a reduction in PTSD symptoms of flashbacks, nightmares, and anxiety by modulating memory retrieval and extinction.[2,3] Any adverse reactions to supra-therapeutic levels of THC are avoidable by titration and education on how to use CBD. My new knowledge that oral THC/CBD ratio administration decreases anxiety in both those with and without clinical anxiety is based upon a previous research study. This study was an open trial of 10 patients with PTSD, which showed that THC alone was safe, well-tolerated and decreased excitability.[3] It is my practice of superimposing CBD on top of THC dosing regimens that appears to manage even better the hyper arousal symptoms of anxiety, stress, and flash-backs of PTSD.

I look forward to the advancement of cannabinoid medicine, and my participation as a clinician and researcher. I am forever grateful for patients like Wayne that inspire me and push my limits in exploring how best to treat pain and the associated suffering of insomnia, anxiety, and depression with cannabis.

With Warm Regards,

Dr. Sana-Ara Ahmed, MD FRCPC
Anesthesiologist & Cannabinoid Medicine Specialist

REFERENCES

1. Neumeister, A., Normandin, M. D., Pietrzak, R. H., Piomelli, D., Zheng, M. Q., Gujarro-Anton, A., Potenza, M. N., Bailey, C. R., Lin, S. F., Najafzaden, S., Ropchan, J., Henry, S., Corsi-Travali, S., Carson, R. E., & Huang, Y. (2013). Elevated brain cannabinoid CB1 receptor availability in post-traumatic stress disorder: A positron emission tomography study. *Molecular Psychiatry, 18,*1034-1040. doi: 10.1038/mp.2013.61

2. Hirvonen, J., Goodwin, R. S., Li, C-T., Terry, G. E., Zoghbi, S. S., Morse, C., Pike, V. W., Volkow, N. D., Huestis, M. A., & Innis, R. B. (2012). Reversible and regionally selective downregulation of brain cannabinoid CB1 receptors in chronic daily cannabis smokers. *Molecular Psychiatry, 17,* 642-649. doi: 10.1038/mp.2011.82

3. Roitman, P., Mechoulam, R., Cooper-Kazaz, R., & Shalev, A. (2014). Preliminary, open-label, pilot study of add-on oral Δ9-tetrahydrocannabinol in chronic post-traumatic stress disorder. *Clinical Drug Investigation, 34,* 587-591. doi: 10.1007/s40261-014-0212

PREFACE

Thank you for picking up this book. Writing this book has been both a trial and a treasure.

I am a man of few spoken words. I figuratively 'lost my voice' as a child as you will see in the following section. The words you are about to read are my attempt to make sense of the PTSD world I live in.

I was diagnosed with post-traumatic stress disorder in 2012; however, I've been living with it since the 70s. I thought what I was going through was normal. I didn't know how really messed up I was until I went into therapy.

Within these pages, you will discover fear, desperation, encouragement, and hope. You will read about pocket puppies, anger, love, suicide, campfires, nightmares, brothers, and dragons. My life is an open book for you to read (pun intended). Writing, for me, is a safe method of getting it off my mind. I encourage you to try it.

Wayne Federation
Husband, Father, Veteran, Author

Table of Contents

Dedication iii

FOREWORD I v

FOREWORD II vii

FOREWORD III ix

REFERENCES xiii

PREFACE xv

INTRODUCTION xxi

Why I Write 1

What's It Like to Be Sick? 3

The Sentinel 5

Peacekeepers' Lament 7

Yet Another War 8

I am a Little Boy 11

PTSD Wife 13

The Dragon, the Tattoo, and the Puppy 16

Alone in a Crowd 19

What Does He Want Now? 21

The Environment and PTSD 23

Pocket Puppy Tale   26

Taming a Dragon   29

Waiting for Him to Come Home   31

Ode to Sleep   34

Abilify Blues   35

On Being Me   37

No Gain with Pain   40

PTSD Christmas   43

Lost and Found   45

The Knife   47

I Wish   47

The Site   48

Why Don't You Work?   49

Who Are We Now?   52

Some Days   55

The Prisoner   57

Good Morning   58

The Man   59

Goodbye, Bro   60

A Walk in the Wilderness   66

Flashback   68

Little Boy Hiding   68

Me-Day   69

I Want to Resign   71

I Have Been Betrayed   73

The Conspiracy   75

Another Night   76

The Journey   78

Don't Walk Away   80

Is It Real?   82

Someone   83

Lost   84

The Change   87

Life Is Doing It Again   89

The Campfire   91

Despair   95

Adrift   96

Sleep   97

False Hopes   99

Even the Snail   101

I Am Not Broken   104

I Am Afraid   106

The Dragonfly   107

Little Miracles   108

One of Those Dreams   110

Memories   111

Redecorating   112

The Rescue   114

It Doesn't Work   115

I am saying goodbye   117

It didn't work   119

Requiem   120

Why didn't you let me KNOW?   123

PTSD is like an octopus   124

How many People Have You Killed?   127

Coping With PTSD   131

She   134

Did I Do It?   137

Fool's Paradise   139

The Game   141

Dad   143

Anger   146

Secrets   149

Why I stopped doing drugs and started smoking
again   151

Where was God?   154

I Know That You are Here   156

Here I am again.   157

A Talk in Time   159

It's a Long Way Back Home   169

RESOURCES
COPE   173

COPE ALUMNI TESTIMONIALS   175

CAN PRAXIS   176

CAN PRAXIS TESTIMONIALS   179

INTRODUCTION
The Fun of Growing Up After Twenty
(Parents do not do this to your children)

I did not mature, gain an identity, become independent, have an original thought, socialize, learn to work with others, or whatever it takes to grow up, until I left home.

My parents provided a roof over my head, a clean environment, clothes, food, and an education. They also provided me with a generous amount of

- Entertainment—hide and seek when my parent's fighting got so bad I had to hide so as not be dragged into the altercation.

- Time to be alone—when guests came over and I was sent to my room.

- Time for self-reflection and creativity—whenever I tried to express my point of view and was told "Children are to be seen not heard" and sent to my room. My need to be heard was somewhat satisfied when I wrote my parents letters and put them under their bedroom door after lights out.

- Pain control—when my father would strike me for not speaking directly to him.

- Leadership opportunities—when my parents' drinking would flare up to another out-of-control discussion and I would gather my brothers and guide them out of harm's way.

- Subterfuge and rebellion—when I cleaned up after the night before, drinking what was left in the glasses on the table or from the bottles, replacing what I took with water before going to school.

- Role modelling—when my father would work his shift in the fire department and then go to the bar before coming home, saying, as he often did, "Do as I say, not what I do."

- Fear and anxiety—whenever I did something wrong and my mother would say, "Wait till your father comes home."

My childhood was entertaining to say the least. I was compelled to constantly walk on eggshells since I didn't know when the next flare-up would happen and whether I would cause it.

As a result, I spent a lot of time in my room, playing with my toys and, later, building models. I would only leave my room for chores, meals, school, and family trips. This heightened awareness of how I affect my world lives in me to this day.

My childhood taught me that:

- I have nothing to say of value; what was bothering me or going on in my life or my opinion was of no interest to anyone else (it was safer for me to be a listener than a speaker).

- I was not loveable.

- I could not trust anyone but myself to survive.

- Feelings only got me into trouble.

- I had no control over my life (life got better when I joined the army).

My mother taught me that all women (except my grandmother) could not be trusted. By putting off the punishment of minor crimes until my father came home, she was making him out to be the ogre and herself, the saint. I could not confide in my mother without fear of retribution when my father came home (I could talk to my grandmother; she was my guardian angel).

My mother lived in the past, could not forgive and did not take responsibility for her own actions. It was only within the last few years of my mother's life that we could exchange the words "I love you" and mean it.

My stepfather taught me that working hard, and drinking was the manly thing to do. Tears, regrets, feelings were not an option. You made your way by being strong, tough, and non-feeling.

He would never admit he was wrong. He thought his form of discipline would make me tough. He thought he was leading by example, but his credibility was wanting. He taught me to drink hard, be stoic, not show pain and not complain, but fight on. I failed to realize I was doomed to follow suit and not smart enough to stop emulating his behavior until it was almost too late.

Despite my entertaining childhood, I learned to love and respect my parents. They were a product of their generation and did the best they knew how.

No matter how I tried, I too failed at many things. After a failed marriage, I met Dianne. She was instrumental in helping me realize that anger, suicidal ideation, substance abuse, anxiety and depression are not normal behaviors of life – they are a result of a condition called post-traumatic stress disorder.

I was reacting to the trauma I experienced during 22 years of military service. And, it appears that having an entertaining childhood predisposes one to developing PTSD, adding further layers of trauma to the disorder.

Remember the child who was not allowed to talk? Well, he joined the army and still didn't have a voice. It was all about putting one's mind in neutral and one's body in gear. Even as an officer, one of the things frowned upon was having feelings, and particularly talking about them.

I wrote these poems to let my friends and family know how I feel, what I'm thinking about and what I'm dealing with. I now share my poetry with you.

Enjoy.

Why I Write

My daughter asked, "Why do you write?"
Truthfully, I thought, I don't know why
In all my grades, I could never get it right
My creative mind was always dry
I was a stutterer and words were hard
Few took the time to listen
I felt invisible, my psyche marred
I was trapped inside and longed to be free

With no thought in their minds of
The words I might say
I became a listener
A talker to few

Friends would pontificate day by day
No words could I get in
No concepts new
And then came PTSD

It's harder to talk when your mind isn't there
It could be drugs, depression, anxiety, fear
There are things I would say
But it's just not fair
Words don't come easily for those you hold near

But writing is a friend
I can take as long as I please
It waits for me faithfully
It never is unkind
Electronic words I can express with ease
Moving them around to say what I mean

When I bestow a poem on someone I care
It's a gift of thoughts, understanding and such
They listen to my words when I'm not there
They give me the attention I need so much

My poems are not all about me
I write to share my understanding
And give my soul sight
So, you can see
What veterans feel, believe, and live

What's It Like to Be Sick?

My daughter asked, "What's it like to be sick?"
I replied, "Just think of everything that makes you tick."

One day you're rested, energized, happy to be glad
The next day, you're angry, sore, and feeling so sad

Your heart, normally silent and proud
Thumps in your chest, heavy and loud

The good sleep you wish to have every night
Is interrupted, shallow, comes when it's light

The food you eat, vegetables and such
May not be eaten, or eaten too much

Energy, eagerness, willingness to do
Is replaced by lethargy, pain, avoidance too

Family and friends who you find so dear
Are reticent, aloof, unwilling to hear

Plans and projects, you want to complete
Are put aside untouched, destined for defeat

Your mind, once so sharp and clear
Is cluttered with thoughts that create fear

The substances you used and liked so well
Are dangerous, addicting and cause you hell

Sunshine, blue skies, good music, and such
Are replaced by pills you don't like so much

The body is willing but can do nothing at all
Your legs are weak and destined to fall

This is only in the morning, I say,
And in the afternoon …

*   Dianne said: When I heard this, I realized what
Wayne was experiencing in such a compressed period. Such
angst! My heart went out to him even more.

The Sentinel

A sentinel sits on the edge
      of an unused field

broken for decades
unable to heal

Once young, productive, proud
      now alone
           sadness a shroud

None can visit—that's fine—for
many years back, a land mine
hurt him.

His friends and owner forever sad
a victim of politics
          gone bad
     sentenced
to solitude
and rust; he prays

Someday people will trust.

*   In 1979 a Greek Cypriot drove his tractor into the Blue Zone in Cyprus to reclaim land that was formerly his. The tractor hit a land mine. Chief Inspector Jack Thurgar from the Australian civilian police force rescued the farmer. A couple of days later, I was tasked with determining the extent of the minefield around the tractor. Using Second World War mine detectors, a section of army engineers and I found and marked a clear path around the tractor. Later, I found out that the entire field was covered in mines. More people were subsequently killed crossing that minefield. The clear lane we marked was wrong. The blue tractor became a symbol of hope for farmers in that region. In 2006, the minefield was finally cleared, and the tractor was removed and returned to its owner. Some 2,318 mines were subsequently found in that field.

6   WAYNE D FEDERATION

Peacekeepers' Lament

A veteran of many things but not of many wars
        I was sent to keep the peace on far distant shores.
Ordered to separate armies, save lives and property
        Our presence to many meant dislocation,
fear, uncertainty

Weapons were for cleaning, inspections, and show
        No fighting would they see, witness, or know
But white vehicles, blue berets, and flags so smart
        Are targets for men with hate in their heart

Ordered to not fire but shout and wave
        Meant little for those we could not save
Peacekeepers … part of the confusion
Not even close to the solution

Yet Another War

I am a veteran of many wars
Some within our very own shores

"We are at peace" you say,
                        but I fight every day

The fight I fight is within, you see,
                a fight with myself
                with PTSD

I fight to stay alert
So those I love, do not get hurt

I fight depression, anger, anxiety
                    to keep myself in reality

I fight the words that race through my
                head, the words that tell me
                I'm better off dead

I fight the sounds, the smells, the faces that
                  send me back to painful places

I have lost my job, my position, my pay
I fight the desire to remain in bed all day

My sense of self-worth, confidence, and play, I fight
              to stop them
                      from slipping away

I must meditate, relax, contemplate
I fight for my wife whose job fills my plate

My counsellors say I'll be
better someday,
for that …

I pray

I am a Little Boy

I am a little boy crying in his bed
All he wants is to be loved, hugged, and heard
       And he is not.

I am a little boy bullied at school
Name calling, shoves and taunts are the rule
       Friends, they are not.

I am a little boy who cannot talk
He has much to say but
       Stuttering makes it naught.

I am a little boy praying for peace
His parents are fighting
       Feeling safe, he is not.

I am a little boy waiting in fear
In his father's court
       Find justice, he will not.

I am a little boy stealing his first drink
I am my father's son, he says
       Sober, he is not.

I am a little boy signing up
He's running away from home now
       Free, he is not.

I am a soldier now carrying a gun
Protecting his home and country
       His enemy, he knows not.

I am a soldier now, hiding from bombs
The higher-priced help are
    Protected; he's not.

I am a soldier now, picking up the dead
This time he was lucky
    They were not.

I am a soldier now, caught spying, staring at a gun.
The gun he is looking at
    His? It is not.

I am a soldier now, striving to save a life
Late on the scene
    His efforts are for naught.

I am a civilian now struggling with life
His wife is leaving him for reasons
    He knows not.

I was a little boy and then a soldier
I became a veteran and now—
    I am lost …

PTSD Wife

What's it like being a PTSD wife?
She replied:

It's like I'm sentenced to life

Problems with anger, love and gin have plagued
him since we've been kin. It took a breakdown
to finally show

What he really needed to know

The fighting and drinking, stuff he did was the result
of times past his mind hid. The army sent him to a foreign
place, and he came home

With war on his face

He's silent, confused, unable to respond. He's angry, sad,
unable to bond. His sleep is plagued with unfriendly dreams
some so bad

He wants to scream

His response to life is not what it seems. He hides his pain
just like his dreams. Outwardly, he puts on a strong face,
but inwardly, his mind

Is having a race

Feelings of uselessness, uncertainty, fear, worthlessness,
anxiety, depression are near. His mind cannot tell what is
real, what is not, when a flashback comes

He begins to rock

The sounds, smells and emotions of war, come forth with power as never before. He relives a trauma for him that is real. I watch, hold him close

Listen and feel

When this happens, there is nothing I can do but provide love, affection, and protection too. He doesn't say much. His words are few. He doesn't think deeply

As he used to do

I am lonely. Lost in my thoughts. I can see him struggling, his mind in knots. He does not like crowds, loud noises too, and the places he likes

Are so very few

He finds it hard to concentrate. Things he does are often late. He packs his day with so much to do and when I come home

He's accomplished few

I try to guide him day by day, to help him heal along the way. PTSD is a disorder, not a disease. It can be managed, and symptoms eased. A wife of a veteran is not a life sentence; it requires

Love, kindness, persistence, and forgiveness

The Dragon, the Tattoo, and the Puppy

There once was a man who was plagued with his past. A soldier sent to foreign places, witnessing death, fear, and destruction. He was lost. One of those forgettable faces.

His dragons were the traumas he hid so well—the skeletons in the closets that rattled so loud, the ones if he weren't careful would drive him to hell, the ones he kept hidden. For he was proud.

Dragons when hidden find a way to get out. They worm their way into your day-to-day living. Anxiety, anger, depression; have no doubt—those dragons are gifts that keep on giving.

The despair of the past is so very strong that suicide, drinking and forms of self-harm come forth in a rage that lasts so long they hide the cause of the inner alarm.

Inking the skin brings a form of pain that makes him feel alive again. Art reflecting the battle within for the world to see where he has been.

A dragon wraps 'round his arm so strong, repelled by a symbol of faith. The yin and yang of a battle fought so long; the tattoo is just a visible trace. Each tattoo is designed with love. A symbol of feeling, a sign from above. Each tattoo is a picture that helps with healing.
He could not go it alone. He had to seek help or fail.

So, with help from his wife and a phone, he gave OSI a hale. With counselling and medications, he started to heal. And bit by bit, he began to feel. But something was missing …

A chance encounter with a dog, a wonderful loveable four-legged friend, brought his mind out of the fog and occupied the time he could spend.

Total love, attention, and adoration; the puppy gave his Alpha these gifts with no conditions to its elation, just asking for kindness, cuddles, and lifts.

They became friends with a bond so tight. Inseparable they became day and night and drew from each other the strength they needed to live another day, their fears unheeded.

There once was a man who was plagued with his past. A soldier sent to foreign places … he fears no more.

*   Occupational stress injury clinic–they help soldiers and RCMP manage PTSD.

WAYNE D FEDERATION

Alone in a Crowd

I am a senior, slightly grey,
hurting

        from everything

One of those faceless
people

        no one looks at twice

I have done many things
successful

        some not

I have served on foreign shores
and returned home with scars

I fought the good fight

        but few care

We go about out our lives gently, not
making waves or thinking out of the

box, not getting too involved it's the norm

I have stories to tell, but no one will
Listen. I am the faceless one

        That no one sees

WAYNE D FEDERATION

What Does He Want Now?

My daughter asked me, "Pops, what do you want now?"
I replied, "Peace and love and brotherhood."

But I was flippant—I don't know how to bring
world peace, and being less than truthful
ruins the mood.

There are many things that I want:
        Using less and giving more
        Stopping the voices that continue to haunt
I want to kick PTSD out the door

I want our leaders to pay attention to what they do.
Cutting benefits to seniors is a dastardly crime
Within their gilded cages, they've lost sight
        of me and you
They too will be seniors—it only takes time

It should be public policy to send our politicians to war
The mother, father and all the children should be the first to
go, and then they'll see … the horror, the pain
        and want no more
And outlaw war, because now they know.

Responsibility should be a public pastime
Responsibility for environment
        for themselves
        and others
Then the world will be in its prime
And everyone would be brothers

We need to stop leading shallow lives

There's more in life than what's on TV

Have you ever stopped to say "Hi" to the homeless?
Given your time to help without thought
of recompense?

My daughter asked me, "Pops, what do you want now?"
I replied, "Peace and love and brotherhood."

I can picture the world as it could be—Wow! —now I
have something to work for that's good.

And I did.

* After many years of self-imposed isolation, I am cautiously venturing forth into the world. As you will see in a later poem, I have found comfort helping others.

The Environment and PTSD

Have you ever been startled by someone behind you?
Try living in a world that constantly goes "BOO! "

The sound of traffic drives me insane
It's the sound of chaos that is my bane

I watch a carpenter at his work
The shot of his nail gun drives me berserk

The crack of a sheet of lumber falling
Is another shot that sends me sprawling

Crowds and their noise are of special concern
I take one look and make a U-turn

There are too many people to watch when it's crowded
the sounds of dangers are enshrouded

Firecrackers …
I will not even mention

The track sounds of caterpillars and such
Are the sounds of tanks and that's too much

TV shows are another point of contention
Gratuitous violence makes me seek protection

Canned meat and vegetables I will not touch
They remind of the ration packs I found so tough

The Boston bombing still feels new
Reminding me of a bombing I went through

And that reminder stayed with me a week
Reliving feelings that made me so weak

To you, these sounds may not be intrusive
But my sounds of war have become obtrusive

Pocket Puppy Tale

My name is Angel,

God sent me to help. I'm not very large but I'm big in everything else. I have a heart big enough to love everyone I meet and an attitude large enough to protect those I love.

I have a duty to serve, love and heal. My first love is my Alpha, who has PTSD. It's my job to be with him always to protect him from himself.

You see, some days he's okay, and other days, depression sets in. It's my job to support him during those dark times and keep him entertained by my antics.

And give him my undivided attention. It's difficult because I'm only six months old. There's a world out there I want to explore, but I wait patiently for my Alpha to show me.

But I digress.

Alphas with PTSD need a lot of attention. They need to be held close, loved, and understood. You see, he's been through a lot of pain and trauma ... and life.

I can't heal him, but I can help. He must learn that he needs to talk about what's happened and what he's thinking about.

I'm a great listener. I don't interrupt

(unless I need to go outside).

The second person I support is my Beta.

Together we support the Alpha, but she needs help herself.

Looking after my Alpha can be hard at times. My Beta needs my love and attention during the hard times too.

I love her so much for looking after my Alpha that I give her extra kisses in the morning. When we're alone, she holds me so nice. But when we're all together, I must be in my Alpha's arms.

For that is the job God gave me—unconditional love to all,

but more for my Alpha.

28   WAYNE D FEDERATION

Taming a Dragon

Whenever you're in a fright and the fright
never leaves, a dragon arises
from deep within

The dragon hides within your mind
holds on to the fear and guards it for you
But sometimes, the dragon fails

The dragon revives and takes you back
to the place you hate most—
its place of birth

The feelings, the sights, the sounds invade
your mind; it's as if you never left, which
you didn't
A dragon born is a trauma unresolved,
an unwanted guest that never leaves
that eats at your soul

To survive, befriend your dragon
Learn what it means, what it wants, how
to stop feeding it

This is one adventure one shouldn't go on alone
the caves and caverns are too deep
If not done well, the dragon
simply goes to sleep

Forgiveness will starve a dragon
It will remove the sting, regret and
fear of the dragon's birth

A dragon that has no fear, no
memory, no meaning is
a dragon gone

A dragon with no purpose
is a dragon no
longer a threat

Work with one dragon at a time
Pick the one you can easily win
then progress with the rest

Eventually, your dragons will be tamed
They will remain dormant
And bother you no more

Until the next time ...

Waiting for Him to Come Home

by Dianne and Wayne

My husband is sitting beside me, but he isn't here
Wounded by his past, his mind is nowhere near

I speak to seek him from where he is hiding
I must call; his mind, it is sliding

Down and down into a vortex of grey
I tried to follow but stopped to pray

I know he will heal but know not how
I get discouraged, my head I do bow

I pray this episode hurts less than the last
I pray he will surface from that far-off blast

He is lost within thoughts of his own
Thoughts of traumas he is loath to own

I call out his name. But he's far from present
With no reply, his mind is absent—I lament

Deep in his mind like so many times past
From years ago, the fears they last

He disappears before my eyes
I try to be patient, kind and wise

Please come back, I cry silently, alone
My quiet tears I hide and moan

Where, oh where, has he gone today
Will he return to me, to play?

Ever again?

I wait for him to come home ...

Ode to Sleep

What happened to the sleep I enjoyed
as a baby?

The sleep I needed as a child
The sleep I tried to ignore as a young adult
The sleep I desperately need now.

Abilify Blues

If you can't sleep; if you're dizzy during the day
        and restless at night, that's Abilify

If you're gaining weight and can't get rid
        of that waist, that's Abilify

If you're anxious about everything and settled
        with none, that's Abilify

If you find your body moving in ways you didn't
        tell it to, that's Abilify

If you're thirsty, hungry, feeling weak or
        confused, that's Abilify

If your tremors tremble and your stomach
        rumbles, that's Abilify

When your partner is ready but your libido
        is not, that's Abilify

When you lose an hour in the day and your friends
        walk away, that's Abilify

When your partner gives you a task and you forget
        or get it wrong, that's Abilify

When you chew on your lip and you're not
        hungry, that's Abilify

When you use the drug, and know
        the above, that's Abilify

*   Abilify is an antipsychotic medicine used to treat
major depressive disorder in adults. It was one of many drugs
I was prescribed until they found one that worked.

    WAYNE D FEDERATION

On Being Me

If I stop to think about all that's going on, my life
       passing like a blink
             and it's all I can do
     to hold on

Age doesn't bother me it's just a fact of life; being
       disabled has set
             me free but I'm not
     free of strife

Freedom 55 was the song; invest in your future
       was the verse; the brokers strung
             us along and greed
     caused the burst

Therapy is a weekly meeting; medications are
       a daily treat; my traumas are not
             retreating; my anxiety
     is still front seat

Pain is my bane; chest pains the worst
       kind; is it a heart attack
             or sprain? Or is it
     just in my mind

My sweetheart is my first love; she's kind
       and caring as can be; she protects me
             like a glove and helps
     me keep my sanity

She helps me when I'm down, holds me
      when I hurt, consoles me when
            I frown and understands
      when I am curt

I have another love, a little angel
      that I know, a gift
            from above that will
      continue to grow

She is my pocket puppy, all love and
      entertainment; she jumps on me
            singing yuppie my Alpha
      my contentment

My life is not that bad, I guess; I have more
      goodness than not; if only I was not
            in distress, I would be
      better off than I thought

No Gain with Pain

Who said no gain without pain?

There are many pains to ponder
>Some within, some without
>Some debilitating, without a doubt

Let's start with the pain of regret

Regret about past deeds and new ones
>The pain of dealing with life in a hurry
>The pain of hurting the few

There is also the pain about tomorrow
>Will I be able to survive?
>Will it bring laughter or sorrow?
>What benefits will I derive?

There is the pain when you doubt yourself

Am I too old, do I still have skills
>Will my disorder leave me on the shelf?
>Will I find work with some of the frills?

There is pain within, buried so deep
The cause of which you are loathe to remember but
when it rises from its sleep, the memory it brings
you wish to dismember
Sometimes the pain gives no reason; it doesn't care
when it strikes; no matter what the season
it strikes wherever it likes

How do you handle a pain that's so strong that it
takes your breath away
            The pain can be short
            The pain can be long
Do you go to the hospital or do you belay?

How often can you cry wolf when you seek help?
            Blood is taken
            Advice is given
The doctor's eyes say you're such a whelp
It's your need to survive that makes you driven

Then there is the pain you live with day by day
The pain that's a constant reminder of a body
            You didn't take care of and now
            You must pay in the body
            You're now confined to

So, what do I gain by living with pain
            Is there a lesson I must learn?
            Is there a punishment for being so lame?
            Are there dues I must earn?

You tell me …

42

PTSD Christmas

by Dianne and Wayne

I don't want to do Christmas this year; my heart isn't in it; it's as if I've something to fear and nothing to prevent it. Most of the decorations remain on a shelf, waiting to be displayed. Maybe Santa will send an elf. I pray he won't be delayed.

There's so much false joy in the air the Christmas songs have lost their meaning; it's no longer about peace and being fair. It's that we must buy happiness that's so demeaning. I bought my gifts to share the wealth; the eggnog's in the fridge. I'll raise my glass to wish your health and hope to cross this bridge.

I've watched the Christmas shows and ignored all the news. As for my Christmas spirit that's as far as it goes.
We went to a caroling service. Music filled the air. Candlelight glowed softly. My heart filled with prayer.

Silent fears were put to rest for someone touched my soul. Hope gently glowed within my chest. My shattered spirit is restored, now whole.

Quietly, gently, the Christmas spirit arrived.

WAYNE D FEDERATION

Lost and Found

I found something today that I never knew was there.
It came to me when someone treated me unfair.

Usually I would sit quietly ignoring the slight.
Today, I didn't. I returned the blight.

I told the offender what he did was wrong,
Left his presence and went along.

It took me some time to settle my thoughts.
I was glad of my response, but my chest was in knots.

A friend told me he thought something was wrong.
He said he liked the way I was (I knew then he
didn't belong).

When I was a child, I couldn't use what I found.
My parents used theirs well but kept mine bound.

Throughout school I was afraid to speak.
My stutter was ridiculed and made to look weak.

When I joined the Army I soon had no fear
As my mind was in neutral, my body in gear.

One would think that after years of being a soldier the
Stuttering would stop as I grew bolder.

It didn't. I learned to listen to other people speak.
My nods of agreement never made me look weak.

Living within one's self is living a curse
When you have much to say but cannot converse.

You listen ad nauseam to other people's tales,
which they like to regurgitate without fail.

It's not that I'm not interested to hear what they say
But, when I try to tell my story, I'm not allowed to play.

That was until today. I said what I needed to say and to hell
with the rest of their day.

* Through therapy, I began to express myself and
found my voice. One friend, who does more talking than
listening, told me he preferred me like I was. Sometime later
I was in a coffee shop with my friend and a stranger started
talking to him. Despite my attempts to join the conversa-
tion the stranger ignored me. Frustrated, I left, stopped, and
returned. I told the stranger directly that he was rude, and
other things, in a voice loud enough for everyone to hear. I
turned around and left again, smiling. I finally found the
courage to do what I have wanted to do all my life.

WAYNE D FEDERATION

The Knife

Silver was the knife
      my father chased my mother with

            Dull was the bayonet blade
                I used in unarmed combat

                    Silent will be the knife
                        I push into my gut.

I Wish

I wish my arm or leg was lost.

Then you would realize what war cost
As you cannot see the mind that I lost.

The Site

Morning mist drifted in.

My squadron was placed around the hilltop
supplied with hot coffee and food through
the evening to keep the chill off.
They had been on guard for 13 hours.
In a few more, we could go back to camp.
I had my gloves on, my container in hand.
The wind blew through the trees as two birds
welcomed in the morning. It would be a fair day.
The sky was blue.

I gave a little prayer then continued with my task, picking
up body pieces.

*   A Kiowa helicopter crashed during night-time re-
connaissance exercises. My squadron was tasked with per-
forming crash-site security. When day broke, medics, the
squadron commander and I were tasked with retrieving the
remains of the crew.

Why Don't You Work?

There are many hidden, behind-the-scenes effects
of PTSD. These are some of them.

"Why don't you work?" a friend asked. "You look pretty
normal to me."

What is normal? I reflect. Is normal the mask I wear daily to
stop people from asking me "how do you feel?" Is normal:

- Staring at my bathroom sink trying to figure out what
  to do next

- The fear I have of crowded places

- Perceiving strangers as a threat; planning my response
  and avenues of escape as I approach

- Being fearful of attack from other people in a
  public washroom

- Wanting to stay in bed and not face the world

- Being told that I grab my sweetheart's arm in a death
  grip some nights and she doesn't complain because it's
  not her throat

- Having nightmares within a nightmare

- Not watching TV news for fear of having
  another flashback

- Taking drugs for the rest of my life to prevent me from
  going over the edge

- Having to resign my job and vocation because I can no longer multitask

- Walking into a room and forgetting why I entered it

- Knowing I have less than a handful of people to talk to about what's going on and most of them are counsellors

- Losing faith in my ability to do most things other than living

- Staring at nothing for minutes at a time without remembering why

- Preferring fantasy worlds to the real one

Who Are We Now?

Who were we before this happened?
Were our lives filled with happiness and contentment?
Were our lives filled with chaos and fear?
Who were we before the world stood still?

When time stopped, and the sickness began
Our minds opened and grabbed all it could
(it had to, to make sense of what was happening
to our minds)
Then closed, and our work began

Repeatedly, our minds play that scene
As if we never left
The sights, the sounds, the smells
Haunt us as our minds bring us back

What did God have in mind for us
When he gave us this curse?
Was it to remind us of our mortality?

The infinity of death?
Was it to protect us?
To keep us from being overwhelmed?

Over time, as the memories
Come back, we relive the trauma
Over and over again
But as our minds slowly analyze the event
Fear slowly gives way to understanding
That we were meant to survive

Who are we now that we have been reborn?
In the strength of the knowledge
The knowledge of what we've been through
Are we better than we were before?

PTSD is a disorder, a disorder of time
The worst things of the world
Have been captured in our minds

It may take us the rest of our lives
To figure them out

WAYNE D FEDERATION

Some Days

On many days, the person you see is not really me
I am suffering from a parasite of war called PTSD
Outwardly I may be smiling and nodding a greeting
Inside my heart is racing and my nerves taking a beating

I can start my day kind, cool and collected
Until something triggers me, and I become infected
From daylight to darkness in an instant of a memory
I become so fearful it scares the hell out of me

Crowds, confined spaces, noises of all types
Cause me to shut down and close up tight
I feel the noise bombard my mind and soul
I long for the day when I can once again feel whole

My concentration is gone; I can no longer decide
What is good for me or where I should hide
My anxiety is at a peak and forces me to feel
That those who want to hurt me are so very real

My flight or flee mechanism has been short circuited
My feel option is no longer connected
My mind perceives that something is wrong
But I do not run, I react, and trouble follows along

These episodes can last from moments to weeks
There are many things that make me bleak
TV, construction, traffic, and trains
Are enough to momentarily fry my brains

Other triggers are surprisingly subtle
The smell of diesel bursts my bubble
Guns, knives, power tools as well
Can bend my mind and make me unwell

I can no longer do everything I want
Common sense is needed to reduce the taunt
I live in a self-induced protective zone
In ever-decreasing circles from my home

The Prisoner

It's a noisy, crowded place out there
Often, for me, too much to bear
Whether a restaurant, church, or coffee shop
Noise is overbearing, does not stop

I turn off my hearing aids
But that's not enough

The noise seeps through, impossible to snuff
Can't wear ear plugs, that's not polite
Making me deaf is not all right

I look for a place I can get relief
Without hiding in my house like a thief
Can anyone tell me where to go instead?
I don't like being a prisoner in my head

Good Morning

I have a list of jobs
    circulating in my mind; like
        TV commercials, they
                never end. Why can't I
                    think of them
            only once? Instead of
        ruminating over them
one by one. I could
    pet my dog but she
        likes to lick my nose.
            Closing my eyes and
                monitoring my breathing
            only gives rhythm to
        the thoughts as they
flow; I think I had
        better just get up.

The Man

I saw a man walking proud down my street today.

His back was straight; his chin was up
His arms were swinging by his side
His hands, however, were tightly clenched

As he passed, I saw his eyes were darting left to right. Was he
looking for something? Looking out?
Did I see stiffness in his gait? Was he in pain?

What stories could he tell?

Goodbye, Bro

I said goodbye to my brother today
Being emotionally numb, I had little to say
Ed was part of my life for sixty-odd years
And I hate myself for not shedding a tear

The send-off was nice—over one hundred there
A lot of people talked to me, but it wasn't fair
They knew me, but I remembered them not
Something in my past has made my memories shot

There were veterans, police, and military
Their wives, sweethearts, friends, and family
To share a eulogy said by Dean
A song by Darren brought tears to our hearts
And made our lives a bit more barren

Ed was a friend to all he met
I remember the smile on Ed's face
When we got in trouble
We would do our mischievous deed
And escape on the double

Raiding gardens, borrowing crab apples
Dislocating outhouses
Adventures we prayed no one knew
Ed started to go bald at an impressive age
At seventeen he was all the rage
Being able to buy from the government store
Made his reputation grow more and more

Being raised by alcoholics was not so fun
So, we watched and learned how we thought
Things were done
We never could drink as much as our parents would
No matter how hard we tried, it never was good

Ed was the big brother we all looked up to
He had looks and girlfriends; I was just looked through
Always fifteen months older than I
Ed always got to do things before I could try

He joined the Navy League, then their band
A year later I came in to give them a hand
He was first trumpet; I was first clarinet
Playing with Ed was fun, you can bet

After that came Sea Cadets and another band
Then came the reserves Army land
We went Signals first, then I left for Provost Corps
It was the first time Ed had no one to care for

When I turned eighteen, life at home got out of hand
I joined the Army but not in any band
The Military Police was the first I'd ever seen
A gun, a car with red lights, and a badge—I was so keen
For eighteen months, I worked as an MP

But I wanted more
Something was missing, so I applied for the officer corps
Ed chose a different way to carry a gun
For him the Edmonton Police was all the fun

Home on leave was a time to share
Experiences, shop talk and why I still had more hair
The joke, we said, with no one listening
Was that I came from a different milkman
Who was just visiting

It was amazing how much our father grew up
When I was gone
He was quieter, more respectful, and easier to get along
The uniforms we wore made him proud
Our talks with him never got loud

Our parents were drinkers so we all got along
Everything went well if we sang their song
We knew what they were like when they got cross
Everything Ed and I believed strongly was up to the toss

We used to hide in our room when
Our parents would fight
Scaring their children was just not right
We'd be as quiet as we could and pretend to be in bed the
thought of them coming filled us with dread
When two more brothers arrived, we'd all hide as well
keeping all four of us safe was a living hell
We would gather together and tell a scary story
So, the noise we heard outside was less of a worry

"Stop your crying or I'll give you something
to cry about!"

(That kids were to be seen not heard was beyond doubt)

"You'd better behave, or I'll tell your dad when he gets home!
Don't you dare make noise while I'm talking on the phone!"

The words I love you or how was your day
Were never heard in our house until we went away
To grandma's house; she was so kind
Saying anything bad about her would never
Cross our minds

When Ed and I got in trouble she knew just what to do
A tea made from poppies she did brew
We sipped our cups, and all became mellow
My brother, my friend, my special fellow

Ed joined the reserves, so he wouldn't miss the fun
Of jumping out of aircraft and firing big guns
As we grew older, our feats became bolder
All part of the life of being a soldier
We did not agree about everything

Sports, guns, and hunting weren't my thing
He believed in a God of fear and retribution
I believe a loving God is the solution

We talked about many things, even argued a bit
We never left, however, without seeing fit
To agree to disagree as was right
Because he was too knowledgeable to fight

I retired in 1990 and went back to school
There were no jobs for a trained killer, I was no fool
Ed stayed with the police a little while longer
Till he found a place to retire way out yonder

I tried to get Ed interested in self-awareness
I sent him books and CDs from all the gurus
He promised to look at them but, in all fairness,
His own interests came first and mine were not to peruse

Ed would often say "Yes, okay" or "that sounds good" This
meant I will do it if I'm in the mood
He wasn't the type to accept advice or something new
Would his life have been better if he tried a few?

WAYNE D FEDERATION

Hindsight is not 20/20; it's more like a curse
The many times I didn't see Ed made his life worse
Once or twice a year was certainly not enough
Now that he's gone, my guilt will be tough

Ed died alone.

He was physically alone but not alone
For our God was by his side
He worked very hard to atone
For all of life's foibles one tends to hide

He was loved by many, a feat not easily attained
A man of respect, joyful not proud
A life in the service of many he maintained
He's smiling up there as he watches from a cloud
We will miss you brother … father … friend

A Walk in the Wilderness

Why Is this happening to me?
What have I not done well?
The other guys seem to be free
What put me in this hell?

Was I not trained to be strong?
Discomfort, pain, and stress
I knew them all, my unit was strong
We could do no wrong
And yet something made me fall

PTSD is a disorder not a curse
There will be days that you will feel lost
There will be days that will feel worse
Recovery, you will find, is worth this cost

There will be times you'll be asked to remember
Even though it will be painful you must tell
What you can
The road to recovery is made
Of the pain you dismember
It's the path you must take; it is part of the plan

The wilderness of recovery is not a place to fear
You'll be guided and prodded and given a shove
You may stumble and fall but recovery is near
It's in wilderness that we learn what we're made of
You will learn to respond and not to react
To see the world in another light
With anger subdued, you will know for a fact
That there are ways to love instead of fight

The wilderness is where we learn character
Instead of comfort
Flashbacks, triggers and hate
Will take time to overcome
But each day in therapy is a victory to report
Change will be hard … but it can be done

*   This poem is derived from the following two lines from a sermon I heard in church one day:
A - Being in the wilderness is where we learn what we are made of
B - Being in the wilderness is where we learn character rather than comfort

Flashback

I had a disturbing flashback last night
I remembered that, when I was a little boy, I sang
in a church choir …

Little Boy Hiding

Why am I here? What did I miss?
Why am I hiding, afraid?
What did I do to cause all this mess?
What price must now be paid?

Me-Day

I am having a "me-day" today
I'm not listening to anyone

This is the day I get my way
No one is going to ruin my fun

I'm waiting for a delivery
They couldn't tell me when it would come

They're going to deliver gravel
Making me stay home until they are done

No one is going to ruin this day
I did the dishes, took out the trash

I must keep the weeds at bay
After that, mow the grass

I have my right leg on a chair
I did something to my spine

The pain is almost too much to bear
Pills don't work, I have no wine

No one is going to take this day from me
I must put the stuff in the garage away

Someone is coming for the electricity
After that I can play

I must take my dogs for a walk
I should not stray

I must watch them around the clock
Or they would run away

This day is all for me
There's laundry to be done and put away

I must get up to water the new tree
There's also painting if I can find the tray

There's recycling to be done
To add to the fun of flitting my day away

No one is going to take this day from me
Except me

I Want to Resign

I want to resign from the human race; there is too much bad out there for me to handle—the noise, the confusion, the blindness is all unbearable.

I no longer want to play.

Why should I continue if I'm not seen or heard? I am but a shadow, meeting many, but not making any impression; just stepped on and ignored.

I want to enjoy my life in peace, but that will not happen. My defenses are deteriorating. Too many things are working their way through, eating at my soul.

I feel crushed.

Burdened by a world that is out of control. I am losing ground. There is too much of them and not enough of me.

I know that I am loved and not alone. As my outer world crumbles, Diannc will be by my side.

I pray that that will be enough.

There are some days like that when medicine doesn't work. Although I was down, I knew I could pull through with the help of Dianne and meditation.

I Have Been Betrayed

I trusted someone

Who didn't do what they said
My morale is so low I could wish that they were dead
(but I won't)

I believed what she said as we were handling my
brother's estate; I didn't realize she was lying
until it was too late—my bad

Someone said what goes around comes around
For her to treat me like she did, vengeance will soon
abound. It won't be mine, but her own

I pray that her actions, taken without compassion, were
planned, not taken too hastily, for then
a thief is born

I will not be the only victim of her abuse for,
once she wins and is set loose, her true nature
will be revealed

The only legacy we leave this life is our honor; hers has
already been taken from her. She will die
a marked woman.

I will not take revenge on this person
She has already done it for me

---

*   I am the executor of my brother's will. Someone tried
to take the executorship from me in court, but failed.

WAYNE D FEDERATION

The Conspiracy

They don't see me, but I see them

        too wrapped up in their own world

I can be sitting at the same table and
Still not be seen
Speaking continually about themselves, they leave

        no time to listen, they smile and feign

Attentiveness but they don't want
To hear what I say
The world revolves around them

I am but a piece of dust in the sunlight
To be tolerated, to be brushed away; it is as if
I do not exist

        it is a conspiracy of blindness

*   I found that few people, both friends and relatives, were interested in what I was going through with PTSD. It was almost as if they were afraid it was contagious.

Another Night

My body was paralyzed
My mind in turmoil
Every nerve in my body firing

There was a lightning storm in my head
My body was hurting all over
Something was trying to remove my soul

I could barely cry out
I was frightened
My sweetheart held me close
I survived

*   I have many nightmares. Dianne knows how to soothe my tumultuous soul. I am so glad.

The Journey

I have had PTSD for over forty years and
        didn't know it; The last three years of therapy
have been a blessing for me; Now I know
        why I was angry, forgetful, suicidal, scared,
and unable to sleep

        PTSD has cost me jobs, friends, relationships;
I thought I was indestructible, the perfect
        husband and friend; Little did I know

I leave my therapist next month as I cannot
        be cured of PTSD; But I have been conditioned
to manage it; I am less afraid of loud noises and
        crowds; My give-a-shit factor is still gone; My
memory still does not work; I cannot deal with
        more than a few things each day.

What I can do is expand my comfort zone; From
        my house to an ever-increasing circle of
safety; With help from my sweetheart, I can
        rejoin the society I fought so hard to protect.

Seek help from those you love and
        trust; You may not like what they say, but
sometimes reality hurts

However, if your therapy is not working for you,
        YOU have the right to ask for change; Your troubles
are special to you; It may not be like others; This is one
        case where one shoe does not fit all.

This is your journey
Live with it
Manage it
Enjoy the result

Don't Walk Away

Don't walk away from someone when you're 35 km
From home with no car or money
I did.

I normally don't walk away but, this time, I had to
I was asked to remember someone and some place
I could not.

How can I explain that my memory was never good?
And today it's even worse? Is it the drugs
I'm taking, have taken? Is it PTSD
Or something else?

I'm embarrassed that I can't remember
But why do people not hear me when I say I can't
I am not being rude, just truthful
I am trying to be me.

The world doesn't hear those who are silent
For some of us, our world lies within
Our minds are in turmoil, dealing
With what we see and hear.

We just want to be alone
With those we love.

*   I was on a job site with a friend of mine. He asked
me to return some equipment he had borrowed but I didn't
know the person he'd borrowed it from. After a heated discus-
sion, I stormed out. It was then that I realized I was stranded.
Not willing to compromise, I walked 20 km before I had to
call another friend to pick me up. That is what stubbornness
does. It can give you a lot of exercise.

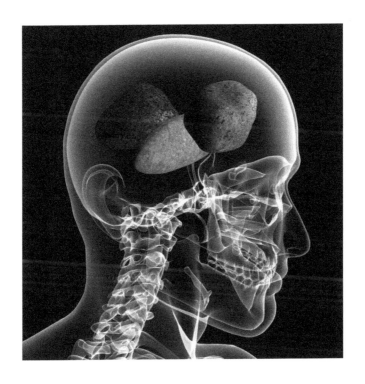

Is It Real?

I'm having memories of events I don't remember
I see an image in my mind
And don't remember being there

Was it a dream, a hallucination or something I forgot?
The image looks real
It's as detailed as any memory, but very short

Is my mind releasing more memories?
After going through three years of therapy
Is it playing tricks on me

Or is it just that I'm getting old

Someone

Someone is banging on my door
There are bright flashes outside my window
Artillery rounds are dropping

But there are no explosions
What the hell is going on?

F... N fireworks

Lost

I've just come to a screeching halt—my phone
won't work, there's no Internet access, I'm cut off
from the world

(There is however an abundance of food and drink here)

I cannot surf the Net, cannot keep abreast of all my
interests; I could go back to long reading but I'm
accustomed to short articles; how can I maintain
interest in one story when there are so many out there
I cannot reach?

I'm going for a walk

What's that, the sound of birds?
Children laughing, people enjoying themselves?
(I don't hear these sounds on the Net)

The sun is so warm; there are waves dancing on
the shore; there are palm trees, swans, iguanas, so
many flowers; the colors are so bright

Nothing like I see on the screen

There are smells of cooking, flowers, the ocean
It's been too long to remember
But I think I used to enjoy being outdoors
The air out here is refreshing
I could get to enjoy this place
Now all I must do is

Find something to do

*   I wrote this poem on a balcony overlooking the ocean in Mazatlán.

WAYNE D FEDERATION

The Change

The world changed quick and silently
Few of us knew it was happening
> People who were normally reserved but friendly
> Became suspicious and dangerous

Places of entertainment were no longer
Shopping centres and crowds became living hell
> Friends and acquaintances disappeared
> Families were torn apart

Those of us who knew became isolated
Some turned to drink or drugs to hide the pain
> Others who couldn't accept it killed themselves
Until they found us, we suffered

Resistance was futile. We had to be re-assimilated
Representatives of those who led us into this
> Catastrophe began reprogramming our brains
> They did their best

Outwardly we looked changed
Inwardly, we know the truth:
> We can never return to our
> Pre-PTSD world ever again

WAYNE D FEDERATION

Life Is Doing It Again

I just came back from vacation

Life has already wrapped its tentacles around me
Pulling me apart in too many directions
With its problems, intrigues, traumas, and worries

My PTSD is not behaving itself
My blood pressure is increasing

I long for a place of comfort and control
Like where I was last week in Mexico
No worries no stress, just sun, food, and drink

My blood pressure was low
My PTSD was sleeping

I think I need to ask my doctor for a prescription
for Mexico

The Campfire

Sitting by a campfire watching the flames
Relaxing in cool fall night, basking in the silence
No worries to be seen, no problems to be tamed
Wondering why my mind remains defiant

I am in recovery, you see, from things
Beyond my control
Therapy and drugs try to define me, but they're not
My heart and soul

Somewhere within this mess lies the real me
Someone with a future and drive, not the shell
Of the person you see, but one
Who wants to survive

Despite all the help I've received, I remain
A veteran on the edge; before me lay two paths that
I perceive—one to containment
The other over the ledge

Failure and defeat are not an option. After all the pain
of discovery I've been through; counselling, testing,
Interviews to exhaustion, multiple pains
And anxieties to construe

Tremors, anger, depression, suicidal thoughts
Numbness, phobias, anxiety, flashbacks as well
The numerous nightmares I have fought have made
My life a living hell

My sweetheart and friends say I'm getting better
I'm learning to believe them to a point

If anything, I have learned to withhold
My actions like a sweater; for all the people
Who helped me, I'm not one to disappoint

For every setback I have, I fall to a higher plane
My healing is progressive, my despair
Is never the same, my failures
Are not regressive

I shudder in public places, dislike loud noises
Have a hard time remembering faces
But always keep my poise.

Multi-tasking is not my game; responsibility is not
Quite there; my sense of achievement is not
The same; my accomplishments are
Sometimes fair

Instead of chasing the mighty dollar, I strive
To improve each day; my realm of influence
Is a lot smaller so I accept what comes my way
I tackle the troubles I can handle and ignore
The ones I can't; I won't dim another's
Candle, because we all have our own slant

I seek refuge with those who are close and leave
Alcohol and drugs behind; I have no need
To overdose as I use myself to unwind

My get up and go has got up and went
Whenever I want to do something
My energy is already spent

Exercise is good for depression, so the doctors say
Not doing any is a transgression so I must get on my way
We have so many exercise machines collecting dust
And laundry—why we bought them is a quandary

The words "we are going to do better" resound around
The house; my mind is in a fetter; my will's
As weak as a mouse

If you measure my motivation, I won't make the cut
What I really need is a swift kick in the butt
As hopeless as it seems, it is really not that way
There's healing in my dreams—
I look forward to that day

WAYNE D FEDERATION

Despair

Plunged into despair
My life I want to end
I failed

A soul now in repair
My link to life, I mend
My dragons veiled

Freedom I decry
Voice loud and free
A purpose renewed

Superiority, do not imply
You wish to die like me
It's not the answer

Ones we leave behind
Deserve not pain
They must know why

Why opens to help
With help, we're not alone
Together, we all survive

Alone in despair I was not
Help was waiting
I needed only to seek

*   I wrote this poem to see if I could emulate the style of a good friend of mine, Ed Brown. I have included two of his poems just because.

Adrift

by Ed Brown

Adrift I cast off into the night
Ready for another emotional sail
Like a small wooden boat tossed around in rough seas

Winds blowing
Waves crashing down what is left of my spirit
Shadows pull and claw at my sanity

Monsters with jagged talons tear at me
Teeth sink deep into my peaceful night
Casting aside any hope of rest and solitude

Battles of death and destruction fought in my dreams
Bitter taste of past horrors plagues my slumber
Off in the distance, a glimmer

A ray of hope in the dark void
A reminder that demons lay only in my past
All I need is to walk to the light

Walk away from the nightmares to a softer place
All I need is to stand and fight
Like a valiant guardian or brave knight

For I am not alone.
For I will bow down no more.

Sleep

by Ed Brown

When my PTSD was at its worst, I feared sleep
It never brought me sweet slumber and pleasant dreams

I was plagued by
Dead bodies lying in a grave
Battles of combat playing over and over in my head
As if on a continuous feed

Many nights I would awake, drenched in sweat
A virus of bad dreams infecting my sleep

But I would not give in
I hung on to what was precious to me

I grasped the little happy moments
Like playing on the beach with the kids
Thoughts of sweet soft touch

With that I walked toward the light
With that I take back my night

*   Ed's book is called *A Soldier's Fortune and Other Poems* published by Agio Publishing House. It's a must read.

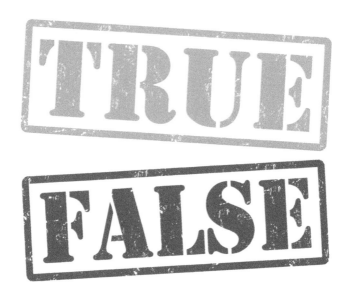

WAYNE D FEDERATION

False Hopes

In a life torn by fear
Desperately I cling to news
Looking for the way
Out of my disorder

Drugs of the 60s
Warned we shouldn't take
Are now okay
(Do you believe?)

Mexico has the cure
An ancient root
The smoke of the gods
If you survive the treatment

Relive your pain
Again, and again
Eventually, you'll forget
(Will you?)

Tap like this
Look this way, that
Engage the full brain
We can hide the pain somewhere

Go away—it will never
Reduce—it probably will
Manage—we can learn how
Live—we most certainly will

Disorder—it is
Disability—it's not
Grow—we can
First step—take it now

Passion—we must find
Work—we must do
For us and more
Higher than drugs

In pain, grow
In fear, learn
Work for you—they will
Better—you become

Go away—it may never
Live with it—we can
Grab it by the horns
Wrestle it down

Make it work for you
You are the master
Of all that is you—
Do something
Be creative
Share your pain
Help others
And help yourself

You can still be
The best you can be
Growth is a certainty
Survive—you can do more

Even the Snail

How can I carry on?
My burden is consuming all
My will to do anything is gone

No energy have I to meet the day
No sunshine finds me inside
Fearing everything, I stay away

Sometimes I stop and stare
As if no one can get through
My body is present but I'm not there

I'm not trying to ignore you
I'm unscrambling my thoughts
So, the one I want can get through

I am easy to anger
But it's not about you
It's my past that is the matter

I have seen things I could not understand
My mind went on hold for my protection
It's now up to me to unravel the strands

Some of the bad things I do
Are from what happened to me as a child
I must ignore what was wrong then and make it new
It may look like I don't love you
I may not be the guy you knew
But we need each other to break through.

Today I did not want to get out of bed
I'm a soldier, I have the will
Thinking of doing nothing filled me with dread

After all I have been through
Having to prove myself again and again
I must get well ... I must do

Even the snail
Had the strength to reach the ark.

I Am Not Broken

Before you stands a person you no longer know
There are things going on within me I can't explain
I may behave in a manner that doesn't show
How much of me that does remain.

My life now is learning how to cope
With everything I once took for granted
I know in my heart that there is hope
I can conquer this gift I've been handed.

I may not do what I did with as much vigor
Crowded places, loud noises, certain sights, and sounds
May cause my mind to react and trigger
A memory of an event I want to keep bound.

I may not seem present—the Thousand-Mile Stare
I'm trying to remember why I'm still there
I may have found something and put it down
Now I can't see it. It cannot be found.

Apologies aren't enough for the pain in your eyes
You are hurt, disappointed, fearful, and mad
Once so young, you are suddenly wise
And know that life is not fair.

You have not lost the one you once loved
I'm still here but my heart has been gloved
I had to hide myself from what I've seen
To come back to you, to become clean.

WAYNE D FEDERATION

You will find me under layers of anger, fear, guilt,
and pain
I am accessible, but it will take time
        With each layer we remove, we will gain
A bit more of me to reassemble.

        Don't let me use PTSD as an excuse to be bad
It's too easy to hide myself and do naught
        Not helping, caring, sharing will make you mad
I am here to protect you, not make you distraught

        I cannot tell you what I've been through
There are things I've done and seen
        I don't wish to trigger myself and upset you
My silence is to protect you, I'm not being mean.

        For me to crawl out my shell
I must participate to reintegrate
        It's not right for me to drag you through hell
I must know my symptoms enough to regulate.

        If I do wrong let me know
I may get angry and tell you to leave me alone
        My anger's not at you; it's my fear of the unknown
The path to rebuild myself is unbeknown
        Together we can do this.

I Am Afraid

I know not why I'm afraid
The task appears easy, I've done it before
As much as I want to it can't be delayed
Tomorrow, I must go into a store

I see no danger, no bombs, nor guns
But my heart is pounding, my chest is sore
There's just people, pastries, bread, and buns
But I can't make it through the door

Across the road, I sit in my car
My sweetheart quietly by my side
I can see the entrance, seems so far
My anxiety soars and I want to hide

"It's okay," she says taking my hand,
"I can come with you if you need me to.
But you must try it alone as planned."
I have no courage, but must make do

I'm out of the car and across the street
I face the door and begin to pull
My heart is willing, but I can't move my feet
And then

… I wake up

*   There is a healing technique that asks one to face
their fears a bit at a time. The thought is, through continued
exposure, one's fears can be reduced. My fear of crowds and
noises makes going into a mall very difficult. I am better if I
am with my sweetheart. If I am alone, it is in and out as fast
as I can.

The Dragonfly

I was out with my ATV enjoying the ride and the dust
When a dragonfly landed on my steering wheel
We exchanged glances

He—it had to be a he for who else would enjoy an ATV
Ride in the dust—stayed there for quite some time
Even though I was driving, he held on

I had a strong feeling that by Brother Ed was near
He passed away last year; the more I looked at the Dragonfly,
the stronger my memory of Ed was

It might be my imagination, but I thought I saw the
Dragonfly smile; then he flew off
Was it Ed?

Little Miracles

Why do we do this to ourselves?
I woke up early this morning and started thinking.
Thinking is nothing new to me;
I do, do it occasionally.

But why is our thinking so rushed at four o'clock in the
morning? I had thoughts
Of what I wanted to do today, things I must do
About my brother's estate

Why am I gaining weight and not exercising?
Can I really afford the new trailer I saw this week?
What do I have to do next in landscaping our yard?
And why did I forget to take a Tylenol?

All this in a split-second, over and over again.
I found one of our puppies and started
Stroking her fur; I calmed down.
Thank God for little miracles.

One of Those Dreams

I had one of those dreams again last night
The one where, no matter what I do, I can't
find my way home.

In this dream, my electronics won't work or they
lead me astray. I see familiar landmarks and they
do the same.

Sometimes, I'm in uniform wandering around
a base. Last night, I was in civilian clothes, wandering
around a city.

I got so frustrated I started crying—waking up didn't
remove the emotion. I don't know why I do this, dream
about being lost.

I know my mind's all messed up with the PTSD drugs,
but I've had this dream since I was a child. Is the dream
a foreshadow of things to come?

Memories

My sweetheart is complaining
About something I have trouble explaining

She asked me a question last night
I couldn't answer and caused a fight

I know my memory is bad
But that's something I never really had

Faces, dates, what I did last week are lost to me
Unfortunate, that is, but it's my current reality

It could be the drugs, it may be the age
But there is nothing I can do to regain the page

Of that memory that may not even be mine

Redecorating

There are days when my meds don't
work and my depression closes in on me.

I could scream
                        but no one is home to listen.

If I break something
                        would someone notice?

What am I trying to say, when I leave a trail of debris
after my anger for someone to see?

Am I exercising my power over my goods just breaking
them because they are mine and I can?

Is this a manly act of ownership and disposal or is it
a childish reaction of being out of control?

Using anger to redecorate your home
                        is not recommended.

*   Recruit locker CFB Cornwallis, Christmas 1968

The Rescue

My demons came back last night
Just like when I was a child
I woke with such a fright
My brain was running wild

I know not why they came
It has been such a while
My drugs normally keep them tame
But last night, they were extra vile

They came from under my bed
My blankets couldn't protect me
I was reeling with dread
Nothing I knew could set me free

Unexpectedly there came an arm
Wrapping itself around my shoulder
Suddenly I knew it meant no harm
The love I felt was making me bolder

My sweetheart rescued me
                                    once again

It Doesn't Work

Separated from the worries
      responsibilities and
life at home
I thought a week in the woods would be
      just what I needed.
      To reinforce
      my need to
      numb out
I started drinking and toking.
The first couple of days
      were fine.
      The sun was shining
      the weather was fair.
      I thought I had completely
suppressed everything.
It didn't work. My anxieties started to
      seep through.
      My worries
      soon followed.
      Then came the pain.
My self-soothing was a failure.
No matter how much I tried to forget
      I couldn't.
      Are my problems insurmountable?
      Life threatening?
I think not.

They are just things I must handle
  when their time comes.
   As much as I tried to forget,
   my problems
   didn't forget me.
Damn it.

I am saying goodbye

I took three handfuls of pills today.
I wonder how long it will take?

I've been suicidal for as long as I can remember
This time is the last. I hope.

I cannot live two lives anymore.
My first life is me. This is the one I must hide.

In my mind, no one is interested in it.
If I try to tell anyone about it, they don't care.

The second life is the life everyone else wants me to live
This is the life I pretend to be. This is not the one I want.

I want to be me. How can I meet others' expectations?
When I cannot even meet my own?

Is there more to life then pretending?
I do not know how to obtain this.

There is so much pressure, so much disappointment
So much pain, so much left unsaid.

I apologize to those who care;
You didn't know how much I hurt
How much you mean to me
How much I will feel your loss.

Take care …

*   I wrote this poem while I was waiting to die. I didn't.
Suicide is not an option; however strong the pain is.

WAYNE D FEDERATION

It didn't work

I'm back, a little worse for wear but okay
I've had suicidal ideation for as long
As I can remember
Then I got so desperate
I tried to kill myself

But I failed …
God is not finished with me yet.

Requiem

It has been a long time since I put pen to paper.

Aren't poets supposed to do well
                              when in despair?

After I attempted the unthinkable and survived
I have been unable, maybe unwilling to write

My mind is in turmoil.
                    What was I thinking?

I would have lost everything and solved nothing
I would have hurt more people than myself

                         Suicide is not painless.

I recently heard someone talk about post-traumatic
growth—apparently there's a future with PTSD; I don't
remember hearing about this in therapy

            Maybe I wasn't ready.

Until now, I thought my future was all about
managing my symptoms. It still is, but I can be productive
         with the right passion.
Shying away from everything that might hurt me
was wrong. Getting out and helping others works.

I am not a changed man
         but I am working on it.

Immersing myself in physical activities keeps
the demons at bay. Aches and pains make me feel
alive. There is a light at the end of the tunnel

　　　　　　and it ain't no train.

WAYNE D FEDERATION

Why didn't you let me KNOW?

"Why didn't you let me know?"

I've heard that phrase so many times.
I failed to kill myself last weekend
and that is what my friends say:

"Why didn't you let me know?"
Why didn't you ask?

When you talked about the last bike you fixed
When you complained about the government
When you discussed all the money you were making

Didn't you see the lost look in my eyes?

Me, clutching the coffee cup so I wouldn't spill it
The one-syllable comments I was giving
My feeble attempts to get a word in edgewise.

I have a right to be heard.

You didn't recognize that when I needed you most
Now you're asking why I didn't let you know

You didn't give me a chance.

PTSD is like an octopus

Its tentacles are
everywhere.
Learn as much
as you can about
the disorder.
Figure out how
it affects you
and your
relationships.
Share this
knowledge with
the ones you love.
Be honest with
yourself and
your loved ones.
Let them know
what you can or
cannot do.
PTSD symptoms
can be managed.
It takes time and
it will be difficult
for you to reach
this state.
Never use PTSD
as an excuse to
be bad or do bad
things to others.
The people who
love you will

understand your
struggles. Let them
know how much
you love them

for struggling
with you.

WAYNE D FEDERATION

How many People
Have You Killed?

My nephew asked me at the dinner table last night:
"How many people have you killed?"

Taken aback I thought:
Why would he ask me that?
Was he really interested in understanding my plight?
Or did he want only the math?

Did he want to know?
That I had the ability to take a life that was dear
Or that I'd dealt that blow
Would he think less of me?

The only life I will tell you I tried to take
Was my own and that was a mistake
My destiny was not to die by my own hand
God was not done with me yet

My life was not so bad
I was still in demand
I've worked over my fears
And reduced the threat

My nephew was speechless
That serves him right
To ask that of a veteran was thoughtless
There are some things that should
Never become known

The next time, I will reply:
"It's not how many I killed but how many I saved".

WAYNE D FEDERATION

PTSD
The Gift That Keeps on Giving

WAYNE D FEDERATION

Coping With PTSD

I have not seen
So much pain, discontent
And angst sitting in one room

Five couples
Who did not know each other
We're bonded by one thing

Couples Overcoming PTSD Every Day
Was the course that brought
Us together

Veterans with trauma
Spouses who have been traumatized
And facilitators who care

Everyone had a story
Very difficult to tell
Some did not want to talk at all

My sweetheart always believed
That PTSD could be cured
After seeing their pain, she saw its tenacity

Talking helps
Shared pains and fears
Builds bonds that weren't there before

Slowly the spouses told their stories
About their journeys
With a veteran with PTSD

It was heartwarming
Despite all the turmoil
The spouses were still there

Some couples talked about commitment
They all talked about pain
There was some talk of separation and despair

We were given an assignment
Our marital journey with PTSD
Each person was to tell their story

It was heartwarming to hear
What each couple went through
In a relationship clouded with pain

As each story was told
And the tears were shed
The couples experienced a bond

There is power
In the knowledge
We are not alone

When the week started
You could feel the tension and pain
That permeated the room

Near the week's end
Couples were holding hands
The transformation was magical

We were no longer alone in our pain
We talked together
And became friends

We were beginning to overcome
The obstacles
That irrational beliefs puts in our way

Communication is the key
PTSD is not an excuse to be bad
You must work on your relationship to survive

We learned that PTSD
Is a family affair
The veteran can't do it alone

As the Phoenix rises from the ashes
We too can rise above
The burden of PTSD shared

She

She was big
She had long hair
She didn't speak
She didn't have to—her eyes said it all

She would follow you if she trusted you
If she didn't, she wouldn't budge
You didn't force her, or she would push back

That could be dangerous

She taught us a lot
She showed us that we had to talk
She taught us the importance of listening

We learned the importance of trust
Of trusting our partners even though their
Ideas and methods may differ

She demanded tranquility
She did not respond to threats or anger
Nor should we

Cooperation is necessary for communication
Anything less than an open sharing of ideas
Is a failure

We learned how to work as a group
To create the environment for learning
And the importance of a bucket and shovel

We mucked out stables, carried water and feed
We talked about our success and failures
We did something we had not done in a long time

We laughed

*   Dianne and I had the privilege of attending Can Praxis, a course in couple's communication using horses. This course is highly recommended. For more information on Can Praxis, please see the special section in Resources at the end of this book.

Did I Do It?

I woke up again this morning with images of a murder
in my mind. This was not a TV movie rehash; there were
emotions within these images.

There is no narrative. I see only flashes of images, the
feelings of pain and fear as I disposed of the body.

I've been told that this is all in my mind, that I have
OCD, that I have done nothing wrong. Why do I feel so
dreadful? I have witnessed death before. My feelings
behind those memories are clinical as I was just
doing my job.

The feelings this morning is different.

> I am attached to this death
> I am afraid
> I must hide the evidence
>
> Where did this occur?
> When did it happen?
> Who is the victim?
> Was I there?

*   Obsessive compulsive disorder (OCD) is one of the
gifts PTSD provides its victims ... to keep them entertained.

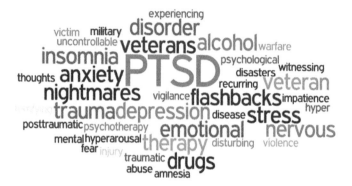

WAYNE D FEDERATION

Fool's Paradise

I'm living in a fool's paradise where
                    fear and foreboding are the norm

Irrational to most, normal to many
I live the life of a person with PTSD

Incurable but manageable I was told
Insidiously ingrained into my entire being
                    I live my day petrified
            When will the next attack come?

                        I am not paranoid.

These attacks are real to me
They come from within with no warning
And a vengeance

Recently my mind told me I
                    murdered someone

With disjointed memories and emotions
I am left with the question

                        Do I turn myself in?

Slowly my world is shrinking as I limit
My exposure from that which may
                    spark a response
        to my past

I choose carefully when and where
I will venture—familiarity reduces
Anxiety as I go forth

Noisy crowded places are worrisome
I cannot hear my assailants
There are too many to watch
They block

                    my routes of escape

          but still I go

If I have no one to watch my six
My trips are in and out
With someone, I can last a bit longer

I don't watch the news
Too much of that reminds me of where
I've been, of memories
                              I wish not to awaken

I have made a commitment, though
To help others

In an environment that is challenging
but stable: the food bank

The work is uplifting
But physically and mentally hard
For every three-hour shift
I need two days to recuperate

Maybe there is
hope for me yet

The Game

With great trepidation, I accepted
An invitation to a hockey game
Remembrance Day eve
At the Calgary Saddledome

I had invitations before
But turned them all down
Tonight, was different
They were recognizing veterans

Crowds, closeness and noise
Make me cringe
But something was happening
That made me go on

They liked us

Wearing the only uniform, I could fit
A circa-1980s garrison tunic
And beret
I ventured forth

My Spidey sense was tingling
I don't like people behind me
I sat in a corner
Trying to control my fears

Then it happened
Strangers were talking to me
Saying how much they appreciated
What we did

This was new
They were sincere
My discomfort reduced
I was safe

Dad

Where were you?
I never knew you
　　　But you were missed

As a child
Your name was mud
　　　What did you do?

Even though
You were not there
　　　I still loved you

Your presence
Was like a ghost
　　　Guiding me on

I always wanted
To be like you
　　　A soldier

When I look
At your pictures
     You seem nice
But you
Abandoned me
     You never called

I found your grave
I had so many questions
     To ask

You were not there
Again
     I was alone

*   My father is buried in the Punch Bowl, a national military cemetery for U.S. forces located in Hawaii. I was very fortunate that day. Many gravestones had been temporarily moved. My father's grave was just on the edge of the area that was being upgraded.

Anger

I am not angry at you
I am angry that I am about to lose control
I'm going to say things that I'm going to regret

You are going to be upset
I may not be able to stop it
I am angry at me

I was trained to handle everything
I had the answers
Everything we did was a drill

We did everything repeatedly
So, we could do it without thinking
even blindfolded

We had a drill for everything but this
We did not have a drill for PTSD
I am angry because they didn't care

They argued that they didn't know
After all the wars, they didn't know
Shell shock, battle fatigue, cowardice

I am angry that there was no plan
To treat us and reduce the threat
Of what was going to happen to us

I am angry that I didn't know what to do
How to overcome what I saw, did, heard, feared
I am angry that I was left to suffer

They let us down, they ignored the past
They deny us benefits, minimize our pain
I am angry at them

I am sorry for what I may say
It's not about you
Even though it maybe you I'm about to hurt

I am angry that I don't know the drill
I am lost, confused, afraid, alone
How do I stop what I'm going to do next?

WAYNE D FEDERATION

Secrets

by Dianne Federation

I'll learn to pretend I don't notice the lies
        the pain behind the smiles
                the tears in the laughing eyes
                     the silent screams
I'll discover my own "home free"
                    inside of me …

Outside, I'll smile
        inside, I'll know
But I have to be careful
                that I don't let it show

It's too frightening for others
And sometimes for me
To "hear" what I hear
And "see" what I see

I can control what I share
        so, others won't see
                the secret sensing and thoughts
                  inside of me

My thoughts are my own
My feelings as well
With these secrets locked inside of me …
Who needs to see Hell?

WAYNE D FEDERATION

Why I stopped doing drugs and started smoking again

I hate drugs
They make you sick
Don't even mention side effects

I used them for everything
Stop me from being so happy
Stop me from being too sad

Stop me from doing everything
No get up and go
It had up and went

Couldn't finish what I didn't start
Being lazy isn't easy
I had to do something

So, I stopped
Cold turkey
(Not a good idea)

Then a miracle
Okay …
A breakthrough

I get to use medical M
Neat
But it wasn't

There's no user manual
No strain guides
It's trial and error

To find the strain
To match your pain

Can't be stoned
All day long
Be the same as using drugs

Some smoke is very strong
For the nose
No good when you're out and about

Some smoke just doesn't cut it
Bad taste, too heady
Never thought I'd complain

But I'll persevere
Now I can get things done
And my sweetheart

Likes me now

Where was God?

Where was God
When the war messed with my mind

Where was He
When I tried to kill myself

Was He listening
When I cursed his name

Where was He
When I lost my faith

It was not until recently
That I found the answers

God was with me on the battlefield
He protected me from severe injury

He was with me when I tried to kill myself
I did not die; He wasn't done with me yet

When I cursed his name
He was sorry I was so distressed

He let me lose my faith
As He knew that I needed him

God was there to help me recover
From the scars of war

He was with me
When I was at my lowest

He showed his love for me
By opening my eyes to his goodness in this world

He showed his faith in me
By giving me strength to help others

He demonstrated his trust in me
When He made me a soldier
And sent me off to keep the peace

He gave me his wisdom
To fight the battles of life

He was there when I experienced success
But I didn't thank him

He was there when
I failed but didn't ask for help

I know now that He is with me
And all of us
He understands veterans

I know this because I thought I didn't have a voice
Before I wrote a poem

I have a difficult time keeping my mind quiet
And yet He gave me the words to write this book

I Know That You are Here

I know that you're here
  But I don't know if you hear me
For you to hear I must tell
  I must tell about my hell

Can I trust you to listen?
  Without judgement
  Without anger
  Without thinking less of me

I have seen things
  I cannot explain to you
I have done things
  I am not proud of

I have served
  But scathed
I have lost parts of me
  That I must find

I don't know what it is
  I am empty
  Afraid, incomplete
Can you help?

Here I am again.

Here I am again.
    The sun isn't shining
I'm awake
    Thinking now what do I do

I could try to go to sleep
    I know I'll toss and turn
    Suffering the chance
    That I will wake my wife

Can't do that

Two of my dogs are with me
I can't let the third one out
    She loves my wife too much
    She will jump on her

Can't do that

I wonder what Trump is up to now?
Should I check?
    And suffer the chance
    Of getting more awake

Shouldn't do that

Political intrigue. Mass shootings
 Tweets, bombings, denials
 Climate change, Fentanyl
 Brexit, Syria, false news

I should have stayed in bed

*   I wrote the following story, A Talk in Time, as part
of my long road to recovery. There was something thera-
peutic in talking to myself by myself. I remember having an
imaginary friend in the form of a teddy bear. Teddy bears
can take a lot of tears without complaining.

A Talk in Time

1.

*[The sound of a child
having a nightmare]*

Me:
Hey, it is all right. You're having
a bad dream.
Think of something else.

My 8-year-old self:
Who are you?

Just a friend.

Why can't I see you?

Because I'm invisible?

Invisible?

I guess you could call me
a dream friend.

I don't think I like this.
Go away.

That's okay. If you ever
want to talk, just call me.
    What's your name?
Wayne.

That's my name.

I know.

How do you know?

I've learned many things
over the years. Can you think
of me as an old friend?

I still don't like this.
Go away.

Okay.

2.

                                  Wayne.
                         You still there?

Yes.

                            Just testing.

Good night.

                         [No response]

3.

                           [The sound of
                          Wayne crying]*

Wayne.
Are you okay?

                                No.
                           Go away.

What happened?

                         Mom and Dad
                         are fighting.

I'm sorry to hear that.
That hurts.

                     [Sounds of sobbing]
                     Make them stop.

I'm sorry I can't.
But I can still help you.

                             How?

We can talk.

                          I'm afraid.

I know.

                  Why do they fight?

There are many possible

reasons. Did
they hurt you?

Not this time.
I'm scared.

You get really frightened at times
and don't know what to do.
Just remember that
even though they fight, in their
hearts, they love you.

That's not the way
I want to be loved.

Your grandma loves you.

Yes, she does.
I like her.

She's a good friend.

She is.

Think of the good times
You have with her and
the pain may go away.

I will.

When will you see her next?

Tomorrow.

Give her a hug from me.
Will you?

[No response]

4.
Hey Wayne.
How are you doing?

Not so good
I'm angry at my mom.

What happened?

She swept up
all my toys.

I can see that would
be difficult for you. Did she
throw them out?

No, she just put them
in my closet.
Said my room was a mess
and that I must pick
them up every day.

That could be a drag.
What are you playing with?

My army toys.
I had made a war
in my room
and she told me
to put them away.

I take it your mother
likes a clean house?

She won't let us play
in the front room.
She says it's for visitors.

That must be tough.
Is there any other place
to play?

Outdoors.
But it's raining.

Have another look at
your bedroom. You may
be missing something.

I don't think so.
But I will.

5.

Wayne.
Are you there?

Yes.
How are you today?

I'm happy.
I found a place
to put my toys.

That's interesting. Where?

Under my bed.
Mom can't see them.
I move my bed, play,
and then put it back.

I'm proud of you.
That's good thinking.
Well done, you.

Thank you.
Thank you for
being so kind.

You're welcome.

[Sounds of sniffling]

Are you okay?

No one said
they're proud
of me before.

Get used to it.
I think you're a great kid.

Aw, thanks.

6.

Hey, Wayne.
How are you

doing today?

I'm okay now. I hurt
my back lifting and
moving boxes.

Ouch. Did you have
someone help you?

No. I like to do
things myself.

Me too.

But after this week,
I'm going to ask a friend
to help me.

It must be nice
to have a friend.

No friends?

I have cousins I play with
but they live
too far away.

Do you have a brother?

I have an older brother.
Ed. But he doesn't like
playing with me.

Have you thought of
hanging out with him?
Find out what he likes and
learn something about it.

What if he says no?

Have you asked him?

No.

Try it. You really can't say
something will be bad
unless you try.

I will.

7.

Wayne.
Why do I stutter?

Are you nervous
when you stutter?

Yes.

What else do you feel?

I feel invisible
and unimportant.

I can feel your pain.

You can?

Yes. I also stutter when I'm
anxious or stressed or
don't know the person
I'm talking to.
I also feel invisible when I can't
join in a conversation.

Me too.
What can I do?

Your stuttering will go away
once you build your confidence.
You must work on building
confidence. Do you play
a musical instrument?

I play the clarinet
in the school band.

And you like the military?

Yes.
My father was in
the U.S. army

but I don't remember
much about him.

Do you know any military
bands you can join?

A guy in school wants me
to join the Navy League.
They have a small band.

Give it a go.
A military band is a great
place to build confidence
and make you visible.
I joined a band when I was
young. I liked the uniform,
the music and the travel.
It helped me gain confidence
and I met a lot of great people.

You know a lot.

Yes, I do.

What can I do now?
Everyone makes fun of me
when I stutter.

Do your cousins or Ed
make fun of you?

Ed's friends do
sometimes.

Let's work with Ed first.
Do you feel hurt?

Yes.

Have you told Ed his friends
are making you sad?

No.

You might want to tell Ed

about his friends. Older brothers
tend to protect
younger brothers, especially if
they know something's
bothering them.

                                   How do you know?

I have three brothers,
one older and two younger.
The older one took me under
his wing and helped me cope
with some of my problems, and
we both helped
the younger ones.

                                   That's nice. But
                             what if he says no?

What did I say about trying?

                                       Oh.
                               Wayne.
                      What else can I do?

You can practice speaking.

                             How can I do that?

Do you like to read?

                                     Yes.

Try reading aloud.

                I can speak to myself okay.
                        It's about others.

I read in front of a mirror.
That way I'm looking at
somebody. When I get nervous,
when I'm speaking to someone,
I look at their mouth. It's less
intimidating than their eyes.

Hey neat.
I can do that.

Do you know anyone else
who stutters?

Jonathan from across the street.
He plays the guitar and sings.

Interesting. How can
he sings when he stutters?

I guess he practices
and likes to sing.

Why would he practice?

So, he can get better.

And so, he can build
his confidence.

Yes, that too.

We talked for another year. My younger self stopped talking
when my parents became too involved in their drinking and
fighting, and their own lives. They still provided clothes,
lodging and food. But what they didn't provide was love.
It took me over fifty years, until I started writing poetry, to
find my voice and the courage to tell the world who I am
and what I feel.

It's a Long Way Back Home

Somewhere on some foreign shore lies

      a piece of me

I don't know when or where I lost it
When I hung up my uniform and was set free
I didn't feel well; I didn't feel fit

I was angry
      I know not why
I drank to forget
      I know not what
I could not feel
      except when I was high

I was emotionally numb … my heart was shut

I worked so hard I made no time to think
Everything was done to excess

    I was stressed
    I lost jobs
    I lost loves
    my life was a blank

I was sleepless, restless, anxious, and depressed

Outwardly, I looked the same
Inwardly, I was a mess

I could no longer feel
      my ability to care was gone
Multitasking caused

too much stress
My problem-solving skills
were overdrawn

A visit to my doctor set me straight
I was ill, disturbed

needed a break

I was sent to DVA to find out what was wrong
Diagnosis of PTSD didn't take long

Years of counselling, medication and not getting high
Dosed with retrospection, inspection, and change
Showed me what was going on and why
And facilitated my life to be rearranged

I learned that my past was real
but it no longer hurts
That I can love without condition and less strife
That drugs can help but they really
pervert the truth about
getting on with your life

Learning to cope with PTSD is only giving in
There's a fork in every road

Choosing the right fork will let you know
Where you've been
Keeping the same path won't lighten the load

Eventually you will know what sets you off and
what you can do to de-stress
For all you've been through, don't get soft

(as is your nature)
continue to do your best

Mother Nature is good for your soul
A puppy or two will help you along
Faith in yourself will help make you whole
Believing in your future will do you no wrong

Each of us has a story that should be told
Your counsellor must know and your friends
        if you're so bold

No one can read your mind; you must say what you need
If you can't say it aloud then pass it to them to read

Learning to capture what's on your mind
Using stories, poems, music, art, and song
Will help you feel less maligned
        no matter what path you're on
PTSD is a disorder, not a curse
It's a long way back home

but it's worth the trip

172

RESOURCES
COPE

COPE or "Couples Overcoming PTSD Everyday" is a new and innovative program that uses the power of the "group" to learn how to manage PTSD in the home. Treating the individual diagnosed with PTSD in isolation misses a major component on the path to better health and a happier life.

COPE is a two-phased program sponsored by Wounded Warriors Canada. Phase One consists of a five-day in-house retreat gathering five couples at a resort to learn together about PTSD and gain new skills to help battle this injury.

This group is led by two trauma therapists as well as a support couple. Together, they help guide this new small community and provide support through the exercises, as couples gain from the personal and relationship experiences. Each member of the couple becomes a "force multiplier"; thus, they gain significant new strength as a couple to move forward towards a healthier and happier life.

Phase Two consists of a six-month family coaching model that employs weekly contact from the assigned coach, who guides each couple in the achievement of their goals set during Phase One. This process continues the learning and practice of new skills, helping to keep the couple focused within their own environment, where the tendency to resort to previous behaviours will be strong.

The importance of the health of the family relative to the path of healing for the injured veteran has been acknowledged by the mental health community but largely ignored in service delivery and programming; the COPE program emphasis on the couple seeks to correct this issue.

If you think you and your partner might benefit from COPE, please visit our website at www.copecanada.ca and fill out the Initial Contact Form in the "Contact us" drop-down menu.

Chris Linford, Lieutenant-Colonel (Retired)
COPE Director

COPE ALUMNI
TESTIMONIALS

"I feel our relationship is actually stronger because we know how to actually resolve conflict and issues rather than just 'waiting them out.'"

"I think we both feel heard and supported by the other now, which I don't think we felt was there before."

"We've used the same conflict resolution skills we learned during COPE with our children and noticed they now use these skills with each other. It's wonderful to see and heartwarming to know that we're setting a good example for them, demonstrating skills that they can carry into the future with their own relationships."

*   More testimonials are available on the COPEcanada.ca website.

CAN PRAXIS

Can Praxis is a three-day program designed for veterans, serving or retired, who have been diagnosed with PTSD or operational stress injury, and their spouse, partner or family member. Couples who suffer the effects of PTSD or OSI will experience increased crisis and conflict in their lives. All activities at Can Praxis are designed to reduce interpersonal conflict and crisis through improved effective communication skills.

The content is divided equally between 1) a critically acclaimed communication and mediation theory designed to promote conflict resolution between spouses and 2) Equine Assisted Learning, a federally-recognized equine discipline that provides participants with opportunities to understand how the horse reacts to their body language, which then becomes a practical segue into conversations that put the theory into practice. Participants walk alongside the horse and do not ride during the initial foundation portion of the program, called Phase I.

The program is conducted by Steve Critchley, a veteran of 28 years in the Canadian Armed Forces, who is also a chartered mediator, and Jim Marland, a registered psychologist with over 40 years of experience in prisons and the treatment of various psychological disorders.

From the outset, the program has been studied by a professional researcher, Dr. Randy Duncan, who is associated with the University of Saskatchewan. His research of Can Praxis has been published in the *Canadian Medical Association Journal* and the *Canadian Military Journal*. The research clearly shows that participants benefit in the short term; Dr. Duncan will conduct a follow-up study to measure the longevity of the benefits. Phase Two and Three will also be studied by Dr. Duncan.

A private Facebook page has been created for alumni to provide sustainable alumni peer support.

Can Praxis is funded by Wounded Warriors Canada; their funding pays for flights (veterans and spouses come from all over the country), hotels, food and programming costs. Veterans do not pay.

Can Praxis has received, and continues to receive, significant interest from the Canadian media and is the subject of a chapter in a recently published book by Stephanie Westlund, PhD.

In addition to the three-day program described above, Phase II involves learning how to ride and care for a horse. This phase is offered by an outfitter and is an opportunity for participants to recall Phase I (in facilitated debriefings), as well as give and receive peer support.

Phase III involves a multi-day horse ride in the Rocky Mountains, supplied by a professional outfitter, and is another opportunity to capitalize on learning and support from the two earlier phases.

Steve Critchley CD
Co-Founder Can Praxis

CAN PRAXIS TESTIMONIALS

Susan Marcotte

I am the spouse of a veteran who has been in the Canadian Navy for 27 years, 18 of which he served as a submariner. He will retire medically this year and we know that this transition will not be without challenges. He suffers from PTSD and has seen military psychologists and psychiatrists for the past four years.

This ONE weekend at Can Praxis was more valuable than all the sessions with the military doctors combined. We both learned many practical life skills for communication and how to look at the coming days with a renewed sense of hope and commitment to work through it all, together. Jim and Steve were the perfect combination, opposites in personality yet both very caring, intent on teaching and listening … often interpreting our unspoken words to be able to direct our thinking and realizations.

They made it feel like a very safe environment, without blame or judgement. Working with the horses was extraordinary. Bonding with our spouse and the other couples there while using the horses to give us immediate and unbiased feedback was incredible.

Without the combination of all these aspects—the setting, the horses, the other couples and, of course, Jim and Steve—I do not think there would be such a great impact. Even though this program is designed to be for people with PTSD and dealing with the fog, the anger and wounds, I highly recommend Can Praxis and the training there for anyone who wants to evaluate themselves and their communication skills and make a plan to move forward in a positive way.

C.J. Wilneff

I'm coming home with a greater appreciation of my life, which, as somebody with PTSD, is a really hard thing to find.

Jacquie Buckley

As I had mentioned to Steve on the phone when I called to enquire about the program, my symptoms with PTSD were managed considerably and all that was missing was my ability to become vulnerable with my feelings again towards my family.

The tools you offered are ones that we can carry forward in our journey as a couple to communicate more effectively through the good and bad times. No words can express how thankful we are for your help, and we look forward to our next steps in this Can Praxis learning journey.

WAYNE D FEDERATION

If you are a budding poet or a short story author, I have an interesting proposition for you. I am collecting short stories and poems from Veterans who have PTSD whether your Military, Police, Firefighter, First Responder, or a spouse thereof. If you are interested, please contact me at wdfederation@me.com. Please add "PTSD Book" to the subject line.

CPSIA information can be obtained
at www.ICGtesting.com
Printed in the USA
LVHW01s0800270918
591483LV00005B/5/P

9 781525 508615